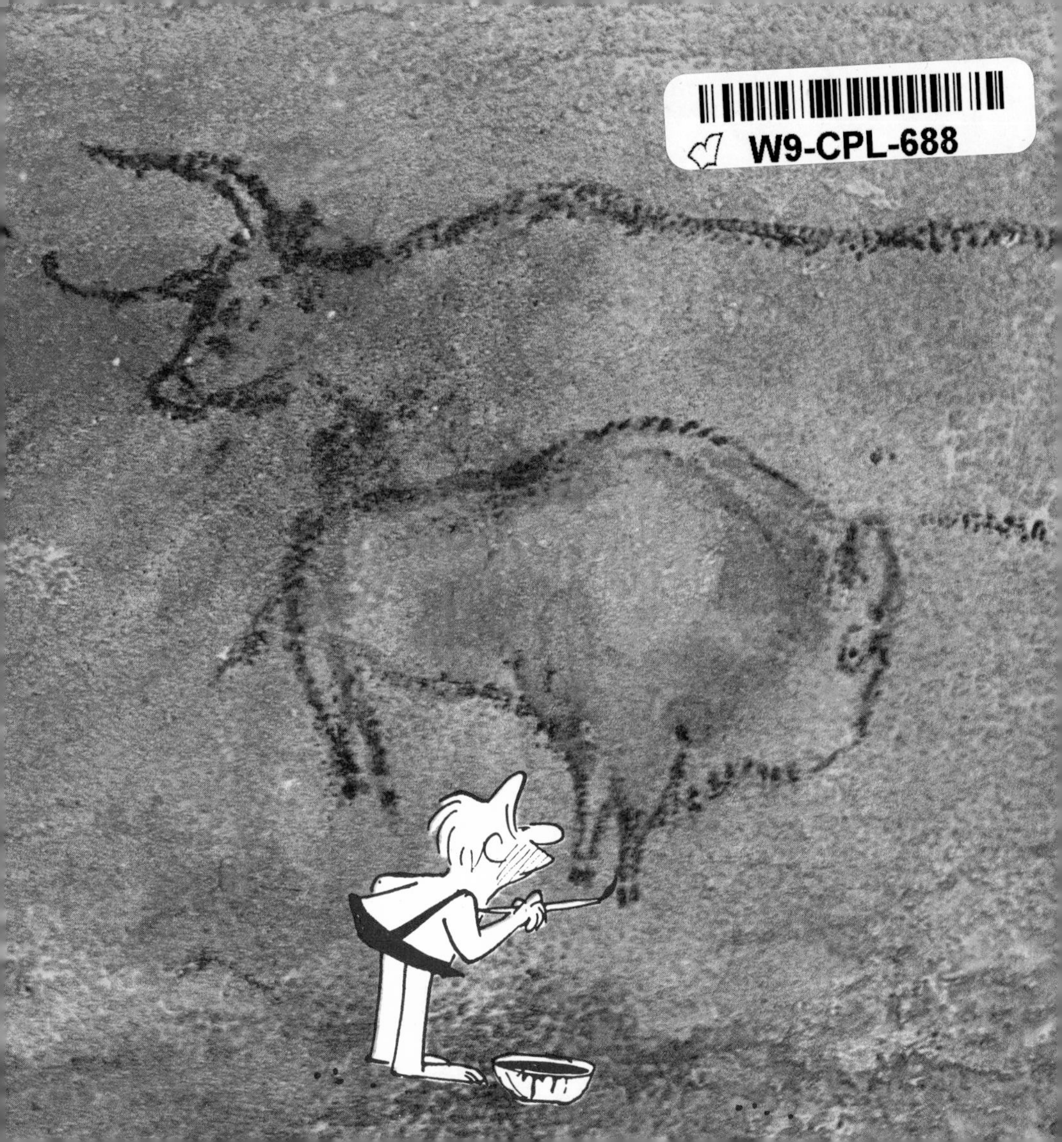

W9-CPL-688

August 24, 1968

With Best Wishes

From

Mark & Celeste Klein

Layout design by Ronald Gratson and Robert Campbell

By Johnny Hart

©1967 AMERICAN GREETINGS CORPORATION CLEVELAND U.S.A.

On the superiority of man

WHAT ELSE ?

WHAT MAKES MEN SO
SURE OF THEMSELVES,
CLUMSY ?

ZAK

GOLLY,...THAT'S HARD TO SAY-

WHAT MAKES YOU MEN SO SELF-ASSURED, AND CONFIDENT?
WHAT GIVES **YOU** THE RIGHT TO PULL THAT **SUPERIOR** JAZZ ON **ME**?

THERE'S A BUG IN YOUR MOUTH.

PETER, ...MAYBE YOU CAN TELL ME, WHAT MAKES MEN SO DARNED SURE OF THEMSELVES?

I'D SAY IT'S INTELLECT; KNOWING WHEN TO COME IN OUT OF THE RAIN.

DRAWING COMFORT FROM THE KNOWLEDGE THAT 2 AND 2 IS ALWAYS 4,-

FEELING SECURE WITH THE WISDOM THAT...
PTUI

On the fiendish plot to dominate man

NOT THAT, STUPID, - I MEAN REALLY MADE OF!
WHO CARES ? THEY CAN KISS!

THE FIRST LOGICAL STEP IN DOMINATING MAN IS TO REACH HIM INTELLECTUALLY.

FIRST YOU PROVE YOURSEL HIS EQUAL, THEN YOU EXHIBIT YOUR SUPERIORITY.

HOW DO YOU DO THAT?

YOU KNOCK HIS TEETH DOWN HIS THROAT.

I CAN'T DO IT! ... I CAN'T BE A PARTY TO THIS FIENDISH PLOT TO DOMINATE MAN.

GET HOLD OF YOURSELF, GIRL! WE HAVE TO GO THROUGH WITH THIS!
SORRY. FOR A MOMENT THERE, I WAS BLINDED BY THE REMINISCENCE OF THOSE BURNING KISSES.

HERE COMES A MAN.
DO YOUR STUFF.

HI, BEAUTIFUL,
HOW ABOUT ONE OF YOUR
UNFORGETTABLE KISSES?

JUST A MINUTE.

THE DOMINATION OF MAN WILL HAVE TO WAIT, – I'M TAKING ONE LAST FLING!